ASK SCARLETT

For Ellie, Eva, and Daisy—*BB*

Copyright © 2026 by Magination Press, an imprint of the American Psychological Association. Copyright © 2026 by National Wildlife Federation. All rights reserved. Except as permitted under the United States Copyright Act of 1976, no part of this publication may be reproduced or distributed in any form or by any means, or stored in a database or retrieval system, without the prior written permission of the publisher. ™ and ® designate trademarks of National Wildlife Federation and are used, under license, by Magination Press, American Psychological Association.

Cover photo credit: (u), dugdax/Shutterstock; (cl), andreswd/iStock; (bl), Sally Cullen, National Wildlife Federation (2016); (r), Max Topchii/Shutterstock

Published by Magination Press in partnership with National Wildlife Federation
maginationpress.org and nwf.org

Distributed by Lerner Publisher Services
lernerbooks.com

Written by Becky Baines
Edited by Katie ten Hagen and Julie Spalding
Book design by Chris Gaugler
Produced by WonderLab Group, LLC
Printed by Versa Press, East Peoria, IL

Library of Congress Cataloging-in-Publication Data

Names: Baines, Rebecca, author.
Title: Ask Scarlett : can being outside help me de-stress? and more questions about nature and you / Rebecca Baines.
Other titles: can being outside help me de-stress? and more questions about nature and you
Description: Washington, DC : Magination Press, [2025] | Includes bibliographical references. | Summary: "In this guide, Scarlett explains why nature helps the brain, how it supports creativity, how it helps kids become planet protectors, and how being in nature and outside has healthy benefits for mind and body!"—Provided by publisher.
Identifiers: LCCN 2024038492 (print) | LCCN 2024038493 (ebook) | ISBN 9781433845246 (paperback) | ISBN 9781433845253 (ebook)
Subjects: LCSH: Stress in children—Juvenile literature. | Stress (Psychology)—Prevention—Juvenile literature. | Stress management—Juvenile literature. | Nature—Psychological aspects—Juvenile literature.
Classification: LCC BF723.S75 B36 2025 (print) | LCC BF723.S75 (ebook) | DDC 155.91—dc23/eng/20241105
LC record available at https://lccn.loc.gov/2024038492
LC ebook record available at https://lccn.loc.gov/2024038493

Manufactured in the United States of America

10 9 8 7 6 5 4 3 2 1

ASK SCARLETT

**CAN BEING OUTSIDE HELP ME DE-STRESS?
AND MORE QUESTIONS ABOUT NATURE AND YOU**

by BECKY BAINES

MAGINATION PRESS • WASHINGTON, DC
AMERICAN PSYCHOLOGICAL ASSOCIATION

Contents

Introduction		7
CHAPTER 1	**Act Natural**	8
CHAPTER 2	**Party Animals**	22
CHAPTER 3	**Sensational Senses**	36
CHAPTER 4	**Wild Weather**	50
CHAPTER 5	**Worldwide Wonders**	64
Glossary		74
Resources		75
Index		76
Photo Credits		79
About the Author, Magination Press, and National Wildlife Federation		80

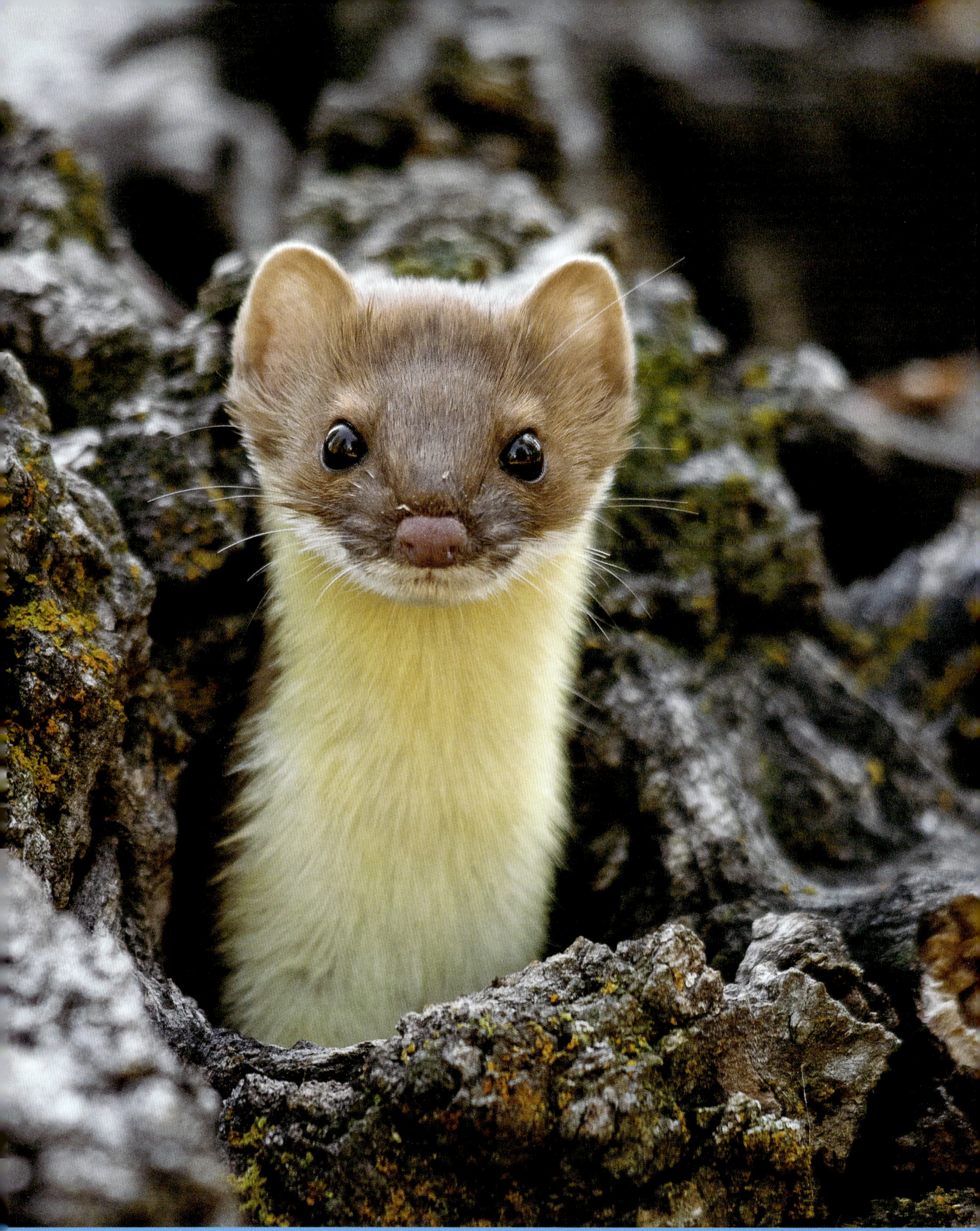

Introduction

Calling all curious kids, inquisitive critters, and anyone else who's just kind of nosy-by-nature...welcome to my book, *Ask Scarlett*, where readers just like you ask me, Scarlett Fox, all their burning questions about nature, animals, the weather, and more! But when I say more, I mean it. This isn't your average Q&A book. This one is all about you!

That's right! In the next five chapters, you'll discover tips and tricks, surprising science, even a health hack or two, all about ways nature affects your mind and body. Learn to sort fact from fiction as we explore everything from how volcanoes give your body a boost to how earthworms make your food tasty. Discover how waterfalls might give your brain a bump, why sunny weather might make you feel happy, why you sleep better in the middle of December, or what rainy weather has to do with good grades. Can a puppy or kitty help you study for a test? Can the color green really affect your mood? What is nature bathing, and why do so many people do it? Can nature really help you de-stress?

By the time you're done reading, you'll be a lean, mean, relaxing machine. So what are you waiting for? Turn the page! Let's get those paws dirty.

CHAPTER 1

Act Natural

Can being outside help me de-stress?

There's no point in beating around the blackberry bush— let's dive right into it!

Getting out in nature can be loads of fun, whether you're camping, climbing, playing sports, or roasting marshmallows over a fire. And having fun helps you feel relaxed and happy. But is there more to it than just fun and games? The answer is yes—and there's lots of science to back it up.

Scientists have discovered that stepping out into the sun for as little as 10 minutes a day can help your body and put your mind at ease. Connecting with nature can instantly boost your mood, make you feel calm, and help you feel less lonely, even if there's no one else around! This is partly because of the chemical effects that being outdoors has on your brain, but also the effects that it has on the rest of your body!

ASK SCARLETT

Being outside affects your **hormones**—the chemical messengers that tell your brain how to feel. When you walk through a forest or stroll on the beach, your levels of stress hormones go down, and your levels of feel-good hormones go up.

And, as weird as it sounds, you sleep better after you've spent time outdoors. You have the sun to thank for that! Studies show that regular exposure to daylight helps support your **circadian rhythm**, the natural cycle in your body that tells you when you should be awake and when you should be asleep. When it's time for lights out—you'll really be lights out! And a good night's sleep is super important for a healthy mind and body! Now if you'll excuse me...YAWN...I think it's time to curl up in my den.

SCREEN GETAWAY

Feeling frazzled? Try shaking up your routine! These days, people spend a lot of time stuck behind screens. Whether for fun—watching TV or playing games—or at school on a tablet or computer, it's hard to avoid! But it wasn't too long ago that this kind of screentime wasn't just a few taps away. In your parents' lifetime, the internet was new technology, and in your grandparents', computers were the latest thing! Research shows that kids today are more stressed out than generations before them. Are screens to blame? Probably not entirely. But it never hurts to step outside for some refreshing fresh air!

ACT NATURAL

Will going out in the heat help me get over my cold?

Runny nose got you down? Unfortunately, there's not much you can do for this one besides wait it out. Despite the popular belief that heat will help you "sweat out a cold," the truth is it's a little too late by the time you're already sick. But, being outside could help prevent you from getting a cold in the first place! That's because soaking up some sun gives you a healthy dose of vitamin D, which boosts your **immune system**—which keeps you healthy. Just don't forget your sunscreen!

Is "fresh air" good for me?

The data is in—and it's a breath of fresh air! When you're indoors, especially in crowded spaces, there's a higher risk of breathing in **viruses** and other germs. These icky particles in the air have less chance of surviving outdoors where people are more spread out. But also, when you're outside, especially moving around, you usually breath more deeply, from your diaphragm—the muscle that sits below your lungs. Inside, where you sit more, you tend to breathe shallowly, from the top of your lungs. And deeper breaths get more oxygen to your brain!

10 ASK SCARLETT

Can rocks heal me?

Lots of people believe that certain rocks and crystals can tap into your body's inner healing properties and unleash lots of health benefits. The idea is that crystals have energy, which they say can be transferred to people. But so far there's not enough scientific evidence to prove that is the case. Still—crystal healing has been practiced by different cultures all over the world for over 6,000 years! Whether or not it really helps, crystals are still awfully pretty to look at!

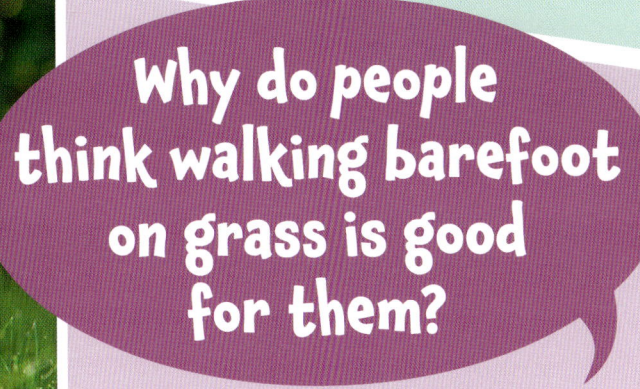

Why do people think walking barefoot on grass is good for them?

Another wild idea is called "grounding"—the practice of walking barefoot on the earth or in water to connect with the electrical charges of the planet. Want to know something even wilder? This one actually works! Scientists measured things like blood cell production and pain levels before and after people practiced grounding. The results show that grounding amps up production of white blood cells, which helps heal aching muscles and fight infections!

ACT NATURAL

Why is the beach so relaxing?

Close your eyes and picture the last time you went to the beach. The warm sun on your skin. The fluffy sand under your toes. The crashing of the waves in the distance. You. Are. Getting. Very. Sleepy. Just kidding! But that's sometimes the effect the beach has on us! It's what experts call a meditative state—when your body is in full relaxation mode, your mind is clear. And there's an added bonus to that clear mind: you are open to new ideas, and your creativity is at an all-time high. So get out there and get to thinkin'!

Why is it hard to breathe when you climb a mountain?

Well for starters, climbing is hard work! But no—it's not your imagination. It is harder to breathe the higher you go. The air is thinner at higher elevations, which means it has less oxygen than lower elevations where most people are used to living. Oxygen is what we breathe, and when there's less of it, our brains get a little, well, fuzzy. You may feel light-headed and dizzy. Luckily, your body is one smart cookie. To make up for the lack of oxygen, your lungs start producing more red blood cells, which are responsible for delivering oxygen to the rest of your body. Your body eventually adjusts, and your oxygen levels return to normal.

Can nature make you nicer?

Being outside can really make you stop and enjoy the simple things in life: the sun on your face, the wind through your fur; and, of course, adorable woodland creatures like me! But those simple pleasures don't just make you feel better. They can help you develop **empathy**. That's right: studies show that time spent basking in the wonders of the wild can make you a more caring friend to people, animals, and the planet. It's also due to the calming effects that nature has on us, allowing us to be present and live in the moment. And partly because of the happy chemicals (**endorphins**) released in our brains when we spend time running and playing outdoors. When we feel happy, present, and fulfilled, it's easier to focus less on ourselves and more on the needs of others.

TREE-TALK

What if I told you that trees are as alive as the baby rabbits that live in dens beneath them—just in a different kind of way? Trees, and all plants for that matter, are living organisms. For the most part, they are self-sufficient, making their own food through a process called photosynthesis, which converts water, sunlight, and carbon dioxide into energy to grow! But it's that very process that makes them so important for life on this planet. Trees provide us with oxygen to breathe, filter the air so it's cleaner, help hold the planet together (literally) by preventing erosion, provide habitats for diverse wildlife… the list goes on and on.

And even though they may not be able to think and feel like critters can, they are a lot more complex than we once thought. Recent studies prove that they even use their vast root systems to communicate and "talk" to other trees!

Soft fur and wiggly noses? Maybe not. Important and in need of protection? Absolutely!

ACT NATURAL   13

Recharge your (solar) batteries

You know the drill—another sunny day at the pool or on the ballfield, and here comes an adult to slather you with sunscreen. It seems you can't step foot outside without someone telling you to wear a hat or stay out of the sun! But the sun is the world's best supplier of good old vitamin D—which is pretty important to overall health. So, what gives?

What does vitamin D do?

First things first—what is it? Vitamin D is a nutrient that helps your body build healthy bones. Your bones are mostly made of calcium, a **mineral** found inside your body and in food, vitamins, and beverages, especially dairy (like milk)! But you can only absorb calcium if vitamin D is present. Vitamin D also helps keep your immune system strong and your gut healthy. Some studies even show if you don't get enough vitamin D, you could start to feel a little down in the dumps. I think it's safe to say this is one vitamin you don't want to miss!

ASK SCARLETT

Where does it come from?

Like most vitamins, you can find vitamin D in some foods, and in supplements if you really need extra help. But your body also makes its own! Much like plants convert light from the sun into energy during photosynthesis, your body converts light from the sun into vitamin D. You grow, you little plant, you!

So is the sun good or bad?

The sun's great! The sun makes the world go 'round—literally. And it's the best source for vitamin D—in small doses. But too much sun without protection can turn your beach day into a beach disaster. That's because the sun is also sending ultraviolet radiation in the form of **UV-A** and **UV-B rays**.

On the spectrum of light, there are rays we can see and rays we cannot. Ultraviolet, or UV, rays fall at the end of the spectrum that is not visible to the human eye. But they're there. UV-A rays, which make up 95% of the rays hitting Earth, penetrate deep into your skin, causing your skin to change color (sun burn or tan) if you are exposed for too long. UV-B rays hit only the top layer of your skin, but they can cause dangerous health conditions later in life. That's why it's super important to wear sunscreen if you are spending time outdoors.

But, Scarlett, how do I get my vitamin D without the damage?

That's a very good question! Doctors say you only need about 10 to 20 minutes of direct sunlight exposure to get the amount of vitamin D your body needs to grow healthy and strong. If you'll be exposed for longer, be sure to take protective measures like waterproof sunscreen (that you reapply every two hours!) or clothing that covers your skin. The rays are strong enough to get the vitamin D you need even through sunscreen!

ACT NATURAL   15

What is "green space?"

What do you think of when you picture your home? A house on a street with lots of neighbors and friends? A camper on wheels that travels from place to place? An apartment in a high-rise in a big city? A cabin in the woods right next to yours truly? For some folks, home is close to lots of nature—for others, not so much. But have no fear, **green space** is near!

Green spaces are nature's "pit stops" in cities and towns. If you're walking along a street in a city amid a sea of buildings, traffic, and noise and suddenly see a beautiful park stretched out in front of you, that's a green space! And technically, so are the bushes around that building, the flowerbeds surrounding that sign, the trees that line the street.

But what's the big deal about a tree? Only everything! First, the air in cities tends to be a little lower quality because of all the people, cars, and industry packed into a tight space. Trees are nature's air filters, removing pollutants in the air and replacing them with fresh oxygen. Plus, plants help to reduce noise pollution, giving your ears a break! They also help deflect heat from the sun back into the air and provide shade, making the ground temperature cooler and providing relief during the hot summer months.

ASK SCARLETT

> **Okay, so if there are "green spaces," are there "blue spaces," too?**

There sure are! **Blue spaces** feature—you guessed it—water! Whether natural or manmade, oceans, lakes, rivers, ponds, and even pools or fountains can provide a ton of benefits for your body.

Of course, there are risks to being around water. It's important to practice caution, wear proper gear, and always follow safety guidelines, especially when swimming, boating, or wading. But that may be part of what makes blue spaces so beneficial for you. Building confidence in challenging places helps you build confidence in yourself as you grow up!

Can the wind make me feel weird?

It's possible that a nice breeze on a pleasant day could be exactly what you need to put you in the chill zone. But could research on some "weird winds" possibly blow in a different direction? Maybe. Depending on where you are in the world, you may have heard of powerful winds like the Santa Ana, sirocco, mistral, or khamsin. People complain of headaches, irritability, and generally feeling unwell when these winds blow. Some even believe that babies become more restless when these winds blow. Although the science is still a little fuzzy, it's possible these infamous winds make people feel bad, because they are packed full of positively charged **ions**. I know you're thinking, *But Scarlett, isn't positive good?* Sometimes, yes. And ions, or groups of atoms with a charge, are always in the air. But when there are too many positive ions (ions with a positive charge), they may make us feel a little bit, well, negative. Scientists don't exactly know why, but some studies show the effects are measurable: Over two-thirds of people tested had higher markers of immune response in their blood when exposed to these positively charged winds. But are the winds to blame, or is it just a bunch of hot air? Experts say there's not enough hard evidence yet to know for sure.

HEALTH HACK
Stargazing can bring you back down to Earth!

Ever feel like the daily dramas of life are bugging you? Maybe you got in a silly argument with a friend or didn't do so hot on a test, and it feels like the end of the world. Here's a quick pick-me-up idea: Go stargazing. Staring at the universe can remind you that you're one person on one planet in one solar system in one galaxy in this whole great big universe. What feels like it's world-ending today might be totally forgotten tomorrow. And this calming effect is scientifically proven: Staring at the stars can lower your heart rate and increase feel-good hormones in your brain.

Can the temperature outside make me moody?

Yes, definitely! Sure, some of it depends on personal preference—you may hate winter, but your best friend may love the snow! You may love basking in the hot weather while your brother or sister cuddles up to the air conditioner with a bag of ice pops! (Personally, I'm a spring girl.) But there are temperature ranges associated with what is called "high" and "low" mood. When temperatures are below 50 degrees Fahrenheit (F) or above 70 degrees F, people experience low mood—feeling off or sluggish. If the temperature is in between those ranges, you may experience high mood—you are ready to roll! Energy levels and exposure to sunlight factor into mood level, too, with energy levels increasing in summer and decreasing in winter, when your body slows down to save energy—kind of like how some animals hibernate for winter (though I've never understood the appeal...).

SOME PEOPLE GET "SAD"

It's pretty common to feel a little down if the weather isn't great. But for some people, it goes further. SAD—**Seasonal Affective Disorder**—affects about 10 million Americans for up to 40% of the year. It usually starts in the fall when days get shorter and peaks in the winter when it's cold and darkness falls early. Then in the summer, you might feel right as rain again. There are lots of treatments, though—including light therapy that mimics the effects of the sun.

ACT NATURAL 19

No Nature? No Problem!

Sometimes it's just not possible to get out to the woods. Maybe you need an instant pick-me-up in the middle of a long school day. Perhaps you're stuck in the middle of a concrete jungle and the green space is sparse. Maybe you're—ugh—sick in bed. There are any number of reasons you could be stuck inside and feeling a little cooped up. Have no fear—nature is nearer than you think! You may just have to get a little creative.

Bring the outside in!

Green space can be anywhere and everywhere. Surrounding yourself with natural elements will bring you that instant boost and trick your brain into thinking you're in the great outdoors. If you're stuck inside for long periods of time, ask the adult in charge about getting some houseplants. Added bonus? Your calmer brain is more creative and better able to focus on the task at hand. More creativity? Now that's something no teacher would argue with!

Open that window!

You don't need to go outside to *be* outside. Sometimes staring out a window is just what the doctor ordered. You get a boost to your mood by looking at nature, and on a not-so-nice day, you're protected from the elements. But if you can, open the window up. The circulation of fresh air will help usher out things like dust, viruses, and even stale smells that might be lingering in the inside air with you. Bonus? Your lungs get a fresh intake of oxygen that gives you an instant brain boost.

Stare at a screen!

I know, I know...I've spent this whole chapter telling you to step away from the screen, and now I'm telling you to go back to it? The truth is that studies show that people who simply looked at images of nature had more relaxing physical responses to tests than people who didn't. That means, when the going gets tough, the tough download a new nature background.

Just add water!

Can't add a green space? Try a blue space. Studies show that not only is the sight of water super relaxing, the sound is, too. So maybe you can't create a fountain where there isn't one or build a beach right in your bedroom, but could you take an extra-long bath or shower? Take a long drink at a water fountain or play with water in the sink? When you do, stop to appreciate the feel of the cool water on your skin and the sound of it as it trickles down your hands. Close your eyes, take some extra deep breaths, and pretend you're at the beach (even if you're just standing in the bathroom)!

Find a sunny spot!

If it's possible to get a seat by a window or open door, do it! Natural light can help minimize the strain on your eyes and improve your ability to think. That's because light is your body's natural signal to tell you it's time to be awake and alert. If you're sitting in a dark corner, your brain may think it's winding down for bedtime, and your mental processes start to shut down. But if you're next to a bright sunny window, your brain thinks the opposite: all systems are go!

ACT NATURAL

CHAPTER 2

Party Animals

Why does playing with puppies make me happy?

Now that's a great question! Everyone knows that we four-legged furry folks are too cute to resist, but dogs are one-of-a-kind. That's because they've been bred over thousands of years to be a human's best friend. That's right—what was once a wild wolf has transformed into about 400 different breeds of cuddly canines, each one with a unique look and abilities. Cats have changed less visibly, but they've been living and adapting with humans for thousands of years, too. What do they all have in common? They have the power to perk up your mood. And I'm not just saying that—it's science!

22 ASK SCARLETT

DON'T TAKE IT PAW-SONALLY!

Not all dogs are party animals—some like their space. Always make sure to ask the owner's permission before approaching a dog for pets.

First, petting animals positively affects those same hormones that are triggered when you are out in nature. When you snuggle a pet, your stress hormones go down, and your feel-good hormones go up. And this love goes both ways—a dog's feel-good hormones go up, too!

Taking care of a pet can give you a sense of purpose and help boost your confidence. Plus, taking dogs for walks keeps you active and gets you out in nature. Dogs are also social creatures, and if you've got a friendly Fido on your hands, you know there's no avoiding interacting with other dog owners. You'll hone those conversational skills in no time!

BEFORE YOU TAKE THAT QUIZ, CUDDLE A KITTEN!

Cuddling a pet can even help you ace a test! More and more universities and colleges have begun to bring in puppies and kittens from local rescues for "animal therapy" before big exams. Studies show that cuddling a furry friend temporarily increases brain activity, which improves attention, concentration, and creativity. Some research shows pet owners get a better night's sleep when their furry companion is curled up next to them (and a good night's sleep is always the best brain boost)! Maybe that's why I know so much—I'm around furry friends all the time!

PARTY ANIMALS

Should I be afraid of bees?

Look, I know. There's something about bugs that really makes people bug out. But here's the thing that bugs me—insects are so beneficial to have around! In fact, some are even necessary for our survival. Take bees, for example. They strike fear in the hearts of picnic-goers everywhere, but without them, there may not be a picnic to begin with. Why? Sure, honey for one (and I do love a sweet treat!), but even more importantly—they are the world's best **pollinators**. When bees fly from flower to flower to collect nectar to make honey, they are also spreading pollen, which helps many plants produce flowers, fruits, and seeds. Scientists think that up to a third of all the food grown on the planet is thanks to bees. And most bees won't bother you if you don't bother them. So next time you see a bee buzzing around your slice of watermelon, think twice before you swat it. It's probably the reason you have watermelon to begin with!

Are earthworms really good for gardens?

This one might surprise you—yes and no! Earthworms work underground, churning up the soil to provide nutrients to help plants grow healthy and strong. And researchers have discovered added benefits to getting wiggly with it—worms can even make your food taste better! Farmers working with worms don't need to add artificial fertilizers, which release nutrients fast but deplete quickly, to their soil. Earthworms working the soil release nutrients slowly over time, producing heartier, more flavorful fruits and vegetables. But there are also many invasive earthworms in the United States, which can actually damage native ecosystems. So the answer is: it depends!

ASK SCARLETT

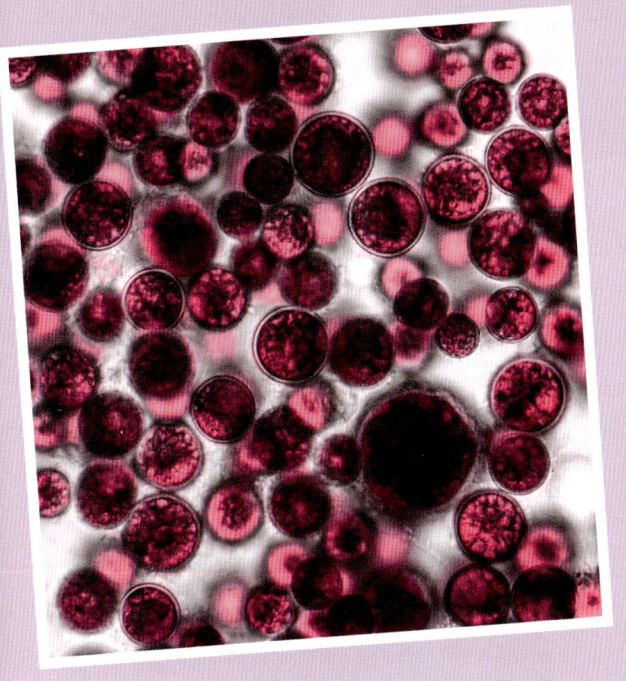

Are there really bugs that live in your body?

Yep—and you should be pretty darn glad they're there, too! You may THINK you would never let a bug within 10 feet of you, but you're about to change your mind on that! The truth is that your body makes a wonderful home to trillions of teeny-tiny microscopic bugs called **microbes**. They may look a bit different from the ladybug outside your window, but these single-cell **bacteria** are still called bugs! They live around and in your mouth, eyes, belly, and skin—just to name a few places. They prevent you from getting sick, help you digest your food, and protect your organs. In fact, your microbes are just as important to your body as your heart and lungs!

DO BUGS HAVE BRAINS?

With 10 quintillion insects (that's 10,000,000,000,000,000,000) on this planet, it's easy to not think twice when you squish an ant or step on a spider. But have you ever wondered if bugs can feel emotion? Do they panic when they're stuck in your window? Do they even have brains? The short version is: yes, they do have brains, and they can be pretty complex. There is even evidence that insects can learn and make decisions. A few can even regcognize human faces. And scientists are just beginning to dabble in research on insects using tools.

PARTY ANIMALS

Can a pet fish make you feel better?

By now you've learned about blue space and the de-stressing effects that water has on your body and mind. And it just so happens that fish live in...the water! So if you have a pet fish, you get the benefits of blue space *and* pet ownership! But here's something you may not expect: Pet fish might actually help kids with diabetes! In one study, scientists discovered that the routine of caring for fish—feeding, checking water levels, and cleaning the tank—helped children with the condition get in the habit of a daily routine. Taking on the responsibility of pet ownership can help prepare kids for all kinds of other responsibilities!

Can bird-watching help me sleep?

There's nothing I love more than kicking back in the grass and watching the birds flutter from branch to branch. Listening to their chirps as soft breezes gently blow...ZZZzzzzzzz...

Sorry about that! Dozed off for a second. That may answer your question, but here are the facts to back it up: Bird-watching engages both your eyes and your ears. Playing a game of I Spy to the soundtrack of tweets and songs gives your body and brain a break from the daily grind. And that brush with nature has a lasting effect: According to research from birding apps, just hearing the sound of a bird's chirp can improve your mental health for up to eight hours, because it tricks your brain into thinking you're in the great outdoors. So how does all this help you sleep? Bird-watching (or even bird-listening) decreases your stress-inducing hormones and improves your mood, and a calm brain is better able to switch from awake to sleep mode. So go ahead and grab those binoculars (or headphones)!

ASK SCARLETT

Is it okay to swim with dolphins?

For decades, companies have been promoting "dolphin therapy" to help people feel better. People have lots of ideas about why swimming with dolphins might help people heal. But after years of research, there's still no hard science to back up these claims. And the practice is not great for the animals. Places that advertise these types of dolphin encounters often keep captive dolphins in less-than-suitable set-ups, which can cause **anxiety** and stress for the animal. And, although highly intelligent, dolphins are wild animals and act like it. People have been bitten, rammed, and even dragged underwater. When it comes to wild animals, it's usually best to appreciate us from afar.

HEALTH HACK
Bust out the baby album!

There's nothing quite like a precious pic of a tiny baby sloth, a cuddly little bear cub, or a fluffy litter of fox kits to brighten up your day. Oops—that's my baby picture. How'd *that* get in there? But would you believe it can help you focus, too? That's right! Scientists studied the effects that baby animal photos had on university students and found that just looking at pictures of cuddly critters helped students do better on detail-oriented tasks. This might be because humans' brains are hard-wired to view babies, all kinds, as helpless and in need of caretaking. Researchers think that after viewing the photos, the part of your brain that cues your need to nurture kicks in, forcing you to slow down and be more careful with your actions. So, next time you need some help concentrating, flip back to this page and look at cute little old, me!

PARTY ANIMALS   27

Hey, Scarlett—what are some ways that scientists learn from animals?

Now *that's* a great question! You might *think* those guys and gals in lab coats are the smartest folks in town. I don't mean to brag, but you'd be amazed what they learn from us out here in the wild world. Check out what just a few of my creature pals are up to!

Naked Mole Rats

Now, I'm not one to judge, but what naked mole rats lack in beauty, they just might make up for in their contributions to science. It turns out these hairless wonders might hold the key to aging gracefully! Naked mole rats have REALLY long lives compared to other rodents—they can live up to 30 years! Mice only live two to three years, and rats usually two to four years. Naked mole rats don't get sick with a lot of diseases that plague their rodent cousins—and humans. And they don't appear to suffer from the same brain and body decline that usually happens as humans and animals age. Some scientists think they have managed to pinpoint one possible reason: Their body produces a high amount of a substance called **hyaluronic acid**, which helps them avoid disease and, in turn, live longer. Can scientists make that happen in humans? That's a problem they're still working on!

Alligators

What's toothy and deadly and might cure an illness? Alligators! Wait, hear me out. Alligators and crocodiles have existed on this planet since the dinosaurs, despite living in harmful environments. The ponds and rivers where they thrive are chock-full

28 ASK SCARLETT

of bacteria and all kinds of yuckiness. That might not seem like a big deal, except these toothy titans inflict wounds on each other often—but rarely get infections. That's because their blood contains unique germ-killing molecules. Researchers are studying whether reptile blood could help boost human immune systems, too. I'll just, uh, let you guys collect those samples…

Arctic Ground Squirrels

The Arctic ground squirrel has a skill unlike any other mammal on Earth. Just like bears and chipmunks, these cute critters hibernate in the winter when food is difficult to find. Unlike bears and chipmunks though, they lower their body temperature all the way to freezing to do so! How? Scientists don't know! It's the only mammal that can survive temperatures that cold! But researchers think that if they can figure it out and copy the process in humans, it could improve treatments for brain injuries. And I thought I was talented!

Kangaroos

You may wonder why female kangaroos, and all marsupials for that matter, have pouches to carry their young. No, it's not just a great way to accessorize! Unlike other animal species, marsupial babies are born before they're ready to survive outside the mom's body. When the baby is born, it stays in mom's pouch, getting nutrients it needs to grow bigger and strong enough for the great outdoors! In the 1970s, when doctors in Colombia were searching for solutions to the lack of proper medical support for newborns in their hospital, they got an idea from kangaroos: skin-to-skin contact! Their idea was that when human babies are born, mom or dad should immediately rest the baby on their bare skin. It helps the baby regulate their heart rate and breathing. And it worked—so much so that now it's used in hospitals around the world. Kangaroos to the rescue!

Sea Turtles

Sea turtle migration was a mystery that stumped scientists for ages. Sea turtles only leave the ocean to find mates and lay their eggs. When sea turtle hatchlings are born, they immediately make their way to the water to live their lives. They may travel thousands of miles in their lives, but always return to the same exact beach where they hatched to lay their own eggs. How do they find their way back? Scientists have long believed it has to do with Earth's magnetic field. Some animals can sense this invisible grid. It seems to be a built-in skill, but scientists never knew how or why some animals had this superpower. Until now! New theories suggest it's actually **magnetotactic bacteria** (teeny tiny organisms that move along the lines of Earth's magnetic field) that live in migratory species that act as an internal compass. Because the research is new, scientists don't know where the bacteria live, or how it works. If the theory is true, though, could humans benefit from it? The jury's still out on this one. But being able to sense your way anywhere? Sign me up!

Octopuses

Octopuses are some of the most intelligent creatures on the planet. They have shown an incredible ability to problem-solve, including performing difficult tasks and even completing complex mazes. But here's a new one: In recent years, scientists discovered that octopuses have a "brain" in each arm. Not a big, round brain like you might be thinking—but two thirds of their 500 million **neurons** (special cells that send messages from the brain to the body) are in their arms. That means each arm has the ability to think on its own. But the arms can also think together as a group. Scientists are studying octopus brains to figure out how to make better **prosthetics** for people missing limbs. Here's hoping octopuses can lend a tentacle on that one!

Hippopotamuses

Have you ever heard the popular myth that hippos sweat blood? (Ew, right?) Well, it's not true. But I get why people used to think that! Hippopotamuses—those deceptively deadly river-dwellers—spend all day baking in the hot African sun. When temperatures soar, the hippos appear to "sweat" a sticky red substance. But it's not blood, and it's not even sweat! (Hippos don't have sweat glands.) It's an oil that oozes from mucus glands to protect them from the sun's harmful rays. And some scientists think it may just be the world's best sunscreen—not just for hippos, but for humans, too. Unfortunately, hippo oil sunscreen presents a few problems: First, researchers have had a tough time testing it, because chemicals in the oil tend to break down before they can get it to the lab. Second, there's the pesky problem that hippos are notoriously territorial, so collecting the oil is not for the faint of heart. And third, scientists think convincing the average person to coat themselves in the sticky red hippo oil might be...hard. Would you do it?

ANIMAL ENGINEERS

Humans have always looked to the natural world for inspiration to make things better or more efficient. Velcro was born when the inventor was inspired by picking clingy burrs out of his dog's fur. The speedy bullet trains in Japan were inspired by the aerodynamic shape of a kingfisher's beak. These sorts of inventions are called **biomimicry**, and it's all around us. But one of the coolest examples of biomimicry in more recent history might just be the Eastgate Centre building in Zimbabwe. Built in 1996, the inspiration for its design came from an unlikely source: termites.

When the heat rises, termites stay cool as a cucumber. How? Their homes are incredibly energy-efficient. Termite mounds are constructed with one large central chimney, with smaller tunnels around the outside walls. While the small tunnels work to ventilate the structure, the internal chimney sucks in fresh air, creating natural air conditioning. The Eastgate Centre building uses the same science on a massive scale. As a result, it uses 90% less energy than other buildings to stay cool! Now that's chill!

PARTY ANIMALS

Can animals understand human language?

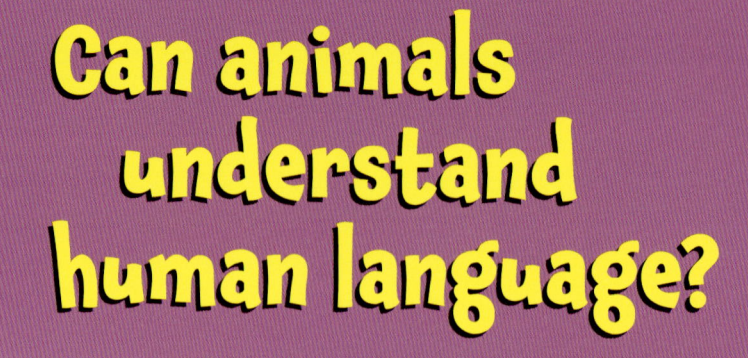

You tell your dog to sit, and he sits. You tell your bird she's pretty, and she might respond, "Pretty bird!" But is it possible for animals to really understand what you're saying? The answer is a bit complicated.

For the most part, when you teach dogs, or any pets, to do tricks or commands, they are responding to the learned behavior of action and reward. You show them how to perform an action, and when they repeat it, they get a treat. If you do this over and over, eventually they will learn: Follow a command, get a cookie. They may not understand the word "sit," but they know that sound and associate it with the action you are expecting.

Companion pets, like dogs, cats, and birds, are smart—that's what makes them easy to train. But really understanding words as concepts outside of cues given to them by humans? Probably not.

You may have seen viral videos on the internet of dogs using buttons to communicate in sentences. It may look as if Fido will call his owner a name if the owner refuses to take him to the beach, but experts don't think that's what's really going on. First, dogs communicate in their own language. Humans communicate in theirs. The button board introduces a third language. Then you introduce other factors like button placement, button color, words, sounds, meaning, context, and more. One expert likened it to a person who speaks English trying to learn how to write in Japanese from someone who only knows French sign language. The viral videos are likely full of trained behaviors and possibly some clever editing.

Still, there are some very intelligent animals, such as gorillas and parrots, that seem to show that animals *can* learn human language. Koko, a famous gorilla who knew over 1,000 different words in sign language, was often pointed to as the prime example. But some scientists and language experts say there was no proof that Koko was able to do more than repeat sequences.

One thing that is scientifically proven? Talking to your pet can help boost your mood, whether or not they understand you. That's right—having a conversation with an animal can make you feel less lonely. They don't judge you, and they can be a sounding board for all your worries and cares. Sometimes, just getting something off your chest is all you need!

Could humans learn an animal language?

If animals can't understand human language—can we try to understand animal language? This is exactly what the folks at project CETI (Cetacean Translation Initiative) hope to find out by breaking down the communication wall between humans and sperm whales.

People have been fascinated by these supersized swimmers ever since they were first recorded "singing" in the 1960s. Now, with the help of marine biologists, roboticists, and linguistics and tech teams, CETI is using underwater robots to track and record sperm whale behavior and speech patterns, creating a huge database of sounds and sequences. One day, the scientists hope, humans can mimic the patterns and "talk" back!

PARTY ANIMALS

Getting by with a little help from your (furry, scaly, hairy) friends!

For decades, dogs have been helping people with disabilities navigate challenges in life. From seeing-eye dogs to help visually impaired people, to dogs that can detect traces of an allergen in their owner's meal, to emotional support dogs that may help people who suffer from anxiety—it seems like dogs have always had our backs! But today's therapy and emotional support animals come from all walks, wags, and wiggles of life!

Miniature Horses

Aside from dogs, miniature horses are the only animals that can be approved as official service animals under the Americans with Disabilities Act (ADA). Service animals are highly trained, have passed all of the certifications and tests, and are legally considered medical support devices. That means they can't be refused entry to any establishment. All other animals fall under the emotional support or therapy categories, but that doesn't mean their services aren't important!

Snakes

An emotional support snake? You got that right! It turns out that the reptile-human bond is just as helpful for some as a furbaby. Although snakes may seem less responsive than dogs or cats, the act of caring for a snake can help build confidence and routine. Also, snakes like to wrap themselves around their owner's arms and hands, which some people say is like a reassuring hug for your hand.

ASK SCARLETT

Llamas

Your feel-good hormones soar when you pet this soft bundle of fur! Llamas are very friendly, giving and receiving affection in the form of soft neck nuzzles. One airport even had llamas on-site to calm anxious travelers during the busy holiday travel season.

Miniature Pigs

These highly intelligent animals provide support to humans suffering from stress and anxiety. And their fine-tuned sniffers can detect danger before it happens. Pigs may be able to detect low blood sugar in owners with diabetes and may even be able to anticipate seizures.

Rats

Experts suggest rats for first-time pet owners in search of an emotional support animal. They're low maintenance, soft and cuddly, intelligent, and fit right in your hands! The touch and feel of a rat can relieve anxiety and stress, and they don't take up nearly as much space as an emotional support llama!

Pet ownership is a big responsibility. As much as you count on the animal to provide you with emotional support, they count on you for everything. Be sure to do some research and make sure you have plenty of support before opening your home to an animal.

PARTY ANIMALS

CHAPTER 3

Sensational Senses

Why do people say to stop and smell the roses?

When someone tells you to "stop and smell the roses," it usually means to take a break from your daily hustle and bustle to appreciate life. And pausing to be grateful for little things sure can turn your Monday mood into a Friday-kinda-feeling. When we foxes say to do it, we mean it literally: Stop and sniff a flower! But can certain scents really make you feel good?

Aromatherapy, the practice of improving your health through scent, dates back up to 4,000 years! It was common in ancient Egypt, Rome, and China to use essential oils (the substance left behind when you crush blossoms, roots, seeds, and leaves) for hygiene, medical, or religious reasons.

ASK SCARLETT

Today, aromatherapy is alive and well, and it's practiced by millions—often using the same plant extracts that were used in ancient times! But what about claims that essential oils can actually heal illness and eliminate infection? The science says there's just not enough evidence say for sure.

So what DO we know? Certain smells have the power to trigger areas of your brain associated with mood and emotion. Plant scents especially stimulate your **central nervous system** and trigger feel-good hormones. And there is some evidence to support that tapping into that power can affect how your brain functions. In one case, kids who took a memory test in a room scented with rosemary did better than kids in an unscented room. Smells promising to me!

SENSIBLE SCENTS

Here are some scents that studies show could perk you up (or put you to sleep)!

Cinnamon = energizing, improves focus

Lemon = calming, perfect for when you're feeling upset

Peppermint = energizing, great for a midday boost

Rosemary = stimulating, gets your brain waves going

Lavender = relaxing, great for helping you sleep

Cinnamon

Lemon

Peppermint

Lavender

Rosemary

SENSATIONAL SENSES

Why does food taste worse when I'm sick?

Having a cold is no fun. Runny nose, drippy eyes, and a cough that makes it hard to get a moment's peace? No, thanks! But the real bummer—even your food tastes blah! But why exactly is that? It turns out your nose is good for more than just sniffing: It's also responsible for about 80% of what you taste! Don't get me wrong, tastebuds also do their thing. But they're only in charge of five tastes: sweet, salty, sour, bitter, and savory. All the flavors in the world—like grape, orange, pineapple, or peanut butter? That's your sense of smell filling in the gaps!

Why does the smell of popcorn make me think of the movie theater?

Have you ever caught a whiff of a something that instantly made you think of a certain person or place? Maybe the smell of freshly baked cookies reminds you of sleepovers with your bestie, a particular perfume brings back memories of a loved one who always wore it, or the smell of popcorn makes you want to watch a movie. It's not a coincidence. Smells are received by a part of your brain called the **olfactory bulb**, which sends the information to other areas for processing. Those areas include the parts that handle memory and emotion. In other words, when your brain smells a scent that's tied to an emotional event, it kind of packages it all together. And scent memories have a huge impact on your mental health! Studies show that smells attached to good memories can reduce stress, increase positive emotions, and improve overall happiness. Now if we could only figure out how to store the smells in the family photo album...

ASK SCARLETT

Does the Earth have a smell?

Trust me, if you've ever caught a whiff of a bear answering the call of the wild, you *know* nature can get pretty stinky. But it's full of good scents, too: blooming honeysuckle, the salty air at the beach...many people can even smell snow. But what about the actual planet itself? Does it have a smell? The answer is yes, it does, and you've probably smelled it your whole life, you just didn't know it had a name. **Petrichor** is the word for the earthy smell after it rains. The term comes from two Greek words: "petra," which means stone, and "ichor," which, in Greek mythology, was the fluid that flowed through the veins of the gods. What causes it? Bacteria. It's always around you, but you smell it more after it rains because the water kicks up bacterial spores into the atmosphere, which make their way into your nose. That might sound a little gross, but humans generally find it to be a really pleasant, comforting scent. As for me? I love it. But then, I sleep on the ground.

Can you smell a happy person?

Compared to the rest of the animal kingdom, humans are pretty mediocre sniffers. To give you an idea, dogs have up to 300 million scent receptors in their noses. Cats have 200 million. Humans are the proud owners of a measly 5 million scent receptors. (Not to brag, but yours truly has about 250 million.) But would you believe that humans can sniff out happiness? This is brand-new research, but experts think that when you're happy, your body may be generating chemicals that come out through your sweat. They call it **chemosignaling**, and although other people may not realize they're picking up your happy chemicals, researchers think they might be able to feel it. It may be that when exposed to chemosignaling, many people may respond by acting happy, too. That means the happy vibes are contagious. Talk about a super-skill!

Can you smell fear? You betcha. The same process that works for happiness works for other emotions, too, namely fear and anger.

SENSATIONAL SENSES   39

Why do hugs feel good?

Hugging can be a great way to feel better! The science shows that a hug from someone you love releases feel-good hormones in your brain. This hormonal rush not only decreases pain but also boosts your self-esteem, slows down your heart rate, and even helps keep you from getting sick! So if you're feeling the love, hug your loved one today!

KNOW WHEN TO HUG IT OUT!

Hugs may be healthy, but only when they are shared in a healthy way. Everyone has boundaries, and knowing when and how to respect them is good for everyone. You are never obligated to give anyone, even family, a hug if you're not feeling it. Likewise, if someone declines your offer of a hug, walk away and hug a tree!

Can your blanket ease anxiety?

Perhaps you're nervous and on edge about something specific. Maybe it's an uneasy feeling you just can't put your finger on. Either way, anxiety can be really uncomfortable! Weighted blankets help a lot of people manage anxiety, because they mimic the feeling of being held or hugged. This is called pressure therapy. Light pressure across your body slows your heart rate, sending you into a soothed, relaxed state. It's the same reason newborn babies like to be swaddled tightly in blankets. Now there's also clothing that can provide pressure just like a blanket, including weighted clothing for people who need pressure therapy on-the-go. They even have pressure clothes for dogs!

Are you ever too old to sleep with a stuffy?

Let's cut to the chase: heck, no! Why would you ever deny your cute and cuddly, soft and snuggly bedtime buddy? In fact, it's possible up to 40% of grown-ups (that's almost one out of every two adults you meet) sleep with a stuffed animal. That's because the benefits are endless! See, your brain doesn't actually shut off when you go to bed. It's still active, just in a different kind of way. Sleeping with your bear bestie can provide a type of soothing companionship that helps you relax so you are better able to snooze. And, of course, there's a sense of security in the familiar. Over time things change; beds, bedtimes, houses. But you can always cuddle up with the same stuffy every night!

Why can't you tickle yourself?

Go ahead—try it! It doesn't work. You might be the most ticklish person on the planet, but no matter how hard you try, it's impossible to be your own personal tickle monster. Why? Because you can't surprise your own brain. When you move any muscle in your body, your brain anticipates the action that is going to occur next. That anticipation prepares your body for the feeling it is about to receive and dulls your body's response to it. If your body didn't do this, you'd be so distracted by the touch or feel of everything, all day, you'd never be able to concentrate.

SENSATIONAL SENSES 41

The Soothing Sounds of Nature

If you've ever scrolled through a sleep sounds app, you've probably seen options like "summer crickets" or "September rain." Nature's symphony can lull you to sleep faster than you can say **hippocampus** (your brain's memory-keeper). Speaking of your brain, let's take a look at how nature sounds affect your body's central command.

➤ **Improves attention span:** In one study, people who listened to forest sounds did better on tests than people who listened to city sounds. The same test was repeated with test-takers alternating between nature and city sounds. They kept performing higher on the sections of the test after listening to the nature sounds!

➤ **Makes you happier:** Here come those happy hormones again! People who listen to nature sounds experience a reduction in stress hormones and a spike in feel-good hormones. That means listening to nature makes you relaxed, less stressed, and happier in general.

➤ **Slows you down:** When humans get stressed out, part of their nervous system kicks in that sends them into something called fight-or-flight mode. This means they either stay and fight, or flee the situation. When that system is in overdrive, it tends to get a little worn out. Listening to bird sounds has been shown to help people recover from fight-or-flight overdrive.

CAN CERTAIN SOUNDS MAKE YOU MAD OR SAD?

Yep—sounds can make you feel any number of emotions! You may hear a particular sound in a scary movie that sends chills up your spine. Or another sound that makes you feel like something exciting is about to happen. That's not an accident! It's our ears' job to listen to a sound. It's our brain's job to decide what it means. Certain tones and pitches of sounds cue certain feelings in your **amygdala**—the part of your brain that deals with emotion. And those feelings are not always positive ones!

SENSATIONAL SENSES

Does the color red make you hungry?

Some people think so! In **color theory**, people believe that looking at certain colors has the power to perk up (or tone down) your day. Warm colors like reds and oranges can energize you and make you feel happy, and cool colors like blues and greens can bring on serenity and calm. Some people think you can use this to your advantage: If you're angry, try staring at something blue. If you're sleepy, try a burst of yellow. And although most people agree there's not enough solid science to back this up, that doesn't stop color theory from popping up in your life every day. For example, many restaurants use red and yellow on their signs, in what experts call the Ketchup and Mustard Theory. Supposedly, yellow and red are happy colors: Yellow makes you feel excited; red makes you feel loved. Together, they might make you want something happy and comforting, and many people associate that with food they ate in their childhood...like hamburgers and French fries. Does it work? Maybe. Hey, is that my stomach growling or yours?

So, what do other colors make you feel? Here's what the believers have to say!

- **Red:** energized
- **Blue:** sleepy
- **Green:** relaxed
- **Yellow:** happy, optimistic
- **Pink:** loving
- **Purple:** imaginative
- **White:** hopeful
- **Gray:** calm
- **Brown:** secure
- **Black:** strong

ASK SCARLETT

Why can something soft and fluffy make me happy?

Did you know it's not just smells that trigger memories, but textures, too? Want me to prove it? Look at any object in the room. Don't touch—just look. Now, imagine what it feels like. You already know, don't you? That's your **haptic memory** at work. Haptic memory kicks in when you feel something on your skin. Your brain records that feeling and stores it away in a sort of mental filing cabinet. Next time you see something of a similar texture, your brain pulls out the memory so you can anticipate what it feels like before you even touch it. Wild, huh? But while you're doing this, your body is also assigning emotions to that feeling. For example, if you love slime, that gloopy gunk sends your feel-good hormones through the roof! If you don't love it, the sticky substance may give you the heebie-jeebies. That's because memories and emotions go hand in hand. What may make one person happy, might make another frustrated.

SENSATIONAL SENSES

Does being hungry really make you grumpy?

Has anyone ever told you you're hangry? You know—hungry + angry? I know I'd rather not be around wolves when they've missed a meal! Hunger is your body's way of telling you it's used up all the energy from your last meal. The amount of sugar in your blood (your blood sugar) is low, and your body's energy source is tapped out. A chemical in your belly then travels to your brain to say, "Hey, I'm empty, what gives?" But when we ignore these signals and continue to go unfed, that's when the hanger steps in. Your blood sugar is also a built-in mood-stabilizing system. With no sugar going to your brain, it's harder to control your emotions or concentrate. It turns out this is a survival instinct seen all across the animal kingdom. When you're starving, there's no space for politeness. But you try telling the wolves that!

Can different foods affect your mood?

Sure can! Now before I dive into this, I'll give you a warning: You may not like what you read. Between you and me, it'll probably prove the grown-ups right. If you're like a lot of people, you probably love to chow down on a good, greasy slice of pizza or dig into a nice sugary bowl of ice cream. And there's nothing wrong with that! Just make sure you're getting a healthy dose of feel-good food, too. *But Scarlett,* you say, *pizza does make me feel good!* Sure, for now. But to feel good longer, you need a balanced diet of protein, fat, and complex carbohydrates (high-fiber things like fruits, veggies, and whole grains). Those other tasty things (sugar, white bread) are simple carbs, meaning they give you a quick sugar spike followed by a crash. When you eat complex carbs, not only do you avoid crashes in your body's mood-stabilizing system, you also get a healthy dose of foods that boost your feel-good hormones. So go on, take a big ol' bite of that pizza pie. Just maybe order it with broccoli on top this time...

ASK SCARLETT

HEALTH HACK
Pack a picnic!

Everything's better in nature! In Chapter 1, I mentioned the benefits of getting outside to send your body into the relaxation zone. When you're dining outdoors, another branch of your nervous system triggers a new impulse in your body. Instead of going into fight-or-flight-mode, it sends you into "rest-and-digest" mode. In other words relax, put your feet up, enjoy a snack! When you're relaxed, it's easiest to engage all five senses at once, each of which plays an important role when you're enjoying a meal. Plus, you get the added bonus of the outdoor feel-good boost while you're chowing down, creating a positive memory across all your senses. Talk about a *sense*-ational meal!

WHAT'S YOUR FOOD MOOD?

Your best friend may love black licorice, and you may think it's the worst thing you've ever put in your mouth. You may think pickles are the bee's knees, but your sister might get sick at the sight of them. We all have the same groups of tastebuds—what gives? It turns out our tastebuds aren't exactly the same.

Tastebuds are located in tiny bumps called **papillae**. And everyone has a different number of papillae. If you have more, food flavors will be more intense. If you have fewer, the flavors will be duller. If you have more than most people, you may be something known as a supertaster! Your tastes are uniquely you. And that's pretty darn cool!

SENSATIONAL SENSES 47

Sensory Scavenger Hunt!

You may have heard someone suggest you go **nature or forest bathing**. No, it doesn't mean taking a tub outdoors! What it does mean is getting outside and using all of your senses to truly take in the environment around you. The green trees above you. The green grass below you. The green caterpillars crawling across green leaves—wait—feels like I'm missing something.

When you simply see with your eyes, you're missing out on nature's feast for all the rest of your senses. Nature bathing doesn't have to mean spending hours deep in the forest. It can be as simple as a short walk. But see how many of your five senses you can use to enhance your experience. When you pay attention to the scents, sounds, touch, and taste of time outside, you'll be amazed how much they play a part in our close bond with nature.

*What to bring:

- A notebook and paper
- A simple snack like berries or carrot sticks

Sight: Using your eyes, find something...

- Red
- Orange
- Yellow
- Green
- Blue
- Purple
- Pink
- Brown
- Black
- Striped
- Round
- Flat

Questions:

Where did you find them?
Did you notice anything surprising?
What was your favorite find?
How did it make you feel?

48 ASK SCARLETT

Hearing: Using your ears, find a sound that's...

- Loud
- Quiet
- Soft and pleasant
- Sharp and unpleasant
- Made by an animal
- Mysterious (you don't know what's making it!)

Questions:
What was your favorite noise?
Did any of the noises bring about an unexpected emotion?
Did you encounter a noise you didn't expect to hear?

Smell: Using your nose, sniff the air. Do you smell anything...

- Wet
- Fresh
- Stinky
- Unexpected

Questions:
Did any of the smells bring back a memory?
Did any of the smells make your mouth water?
Did any of the smells cause an unexpected physical reaction?

Taste: Eat your snack. Notice...

- The taste on your tongue
- The texture as you bite down
- The sounds as you chew
- How your mouth waters

Questions:
Did it taste any different than usual?
Did the taste change as you ate it?
Did it make you think of anything?

Touch: Using your fingertips, find something...

- Soft
- Rough
- Sticky
- Smooth
- Wet
- Bumpy

Questions:
Did anything make you feel happy?
Did anything make you feel sad?
Did anything make you feel soothed?

***Scarlett's Words of Wisdom:** Grab a grown-up before you go on your sensory adventure! Give animals plenty of space, and never touch a plant unless you know it is safe to do so. Oh—and never, ever put anything from nature in your mouth unless an expert tells you it's okay to do so.

SENSATIONAL SENSES

CHAPTER 4

Wild Weather

Can rain make me feel good?

We've all been there: You open the door to head out for the day only to discover—*uh-oh*—better go back and get your umbrella. There's nothing like a rainy day to ruin your plans. Well, what if I told you it might actually be good for you to run through the raindrops instead of running for cover?

Back in Chapter 1 we talked about how some winds may make you feel a little off because they are charged with positive ions. Well, rain is the opposite. When the tiny droplets hit the ground, they pick up negative ions, which have a positive effect on your mental health. Some experts believe these invisible molecules give your brain an instant oxygen boost, helping you feel alert and energized. Others think the science is a little, well, watery, and more research is needed. Still, there's no denying some sort of connection between rain and brain bliss.

50 ASK SCARLETT

Also, like a power-wash for the great outdoors, rain cleans the air, ridding it of pesky **particle pollution** that makes you feel blah. Also, there's the petrichor effect. Remember petrichor, the smell of earth after it rains that humans go nuts for? Well, it turns out it contains a chemical that has an instant calming effect for your brain. They even put it in some perfumes!

Finally, rain works like a lullaby for your mind. Repetitive sounds and touch, like the pitter-patter of raindrops on the trees and the rhythmic feel of drops on your skin, send your brain into a kind of meditative state, sort of like letting waves at the beach gently lap at your feet. So next time the forecast calls for rain, don't run inside. Go for a walk instead. Your body might thank you!

WHY DO SOME PEOPLE GET HEADACHES WHEN IT STORMS?

When a storm moves in, the pressure in the air (**barometric pressure**) suddenly drops, which can have all sorts of effects on your body. Because the pressure in the air changes, so does pressure in your sinus cavities, which are filled with air, which in turn can cause a headache. The change in pressure doesn't have to be dramatic; even a small shift can cause it. But people who suffer from weather-related headaches are often also affected when flying in airplanes, where pressure in the cabin shifts dramatically and quickly.

WILD WEATHER 51

Why do some people say they can feel a storm in their bones?

You may have heard grown-ups say this. So, do adults have some superpower kids don't? Maybe, but the science is still too fuzzy to know for sure. Two things happen before and during a storm. The barometric pressure drops, and the humidity, or level of moisture in the atmosphere, rises. The bigger the change, the bigger the storm. And these changes can take a toll on your body. Science shows that barometric pressure doesn't just affect your head. It also has a strange effect on the fluid in your joints (like your knees and elbows). So older folks who suffer from joint pain may feel it when the temperature is cooler. And if the humidity is higher, people report more pain, though scientists aren't certain why. But internet searches for pain relief go up when weather is bad, so it doesn't seem to be a coincidence. The problem is that there are too many other factors, like behavior, activity level, and environment to account for, so there's no solid explanation—yet!

Is snow safe to eat?

The truth is, fresh fallen snow could safely be consumed directly from the sky to your tongue or even used in ice cream, but once it hits the ground, you have no idea what other chemicals or bacteria get mixed in. Any layer coming into contact with the ground could have picked up bug-repelling pesticides or fertilizer. Snow on top of a parking lot, cars, or concrete can have things like rock salt, carbon, and other chemicals to worry about. And of course, us animals, well... Don't forget we do our business in the great outdoors. They tell you to stay away from the yellow snow for a reason...Don't say I didn't warn you!

ASK SCARLETT

Is mud really good for my skin?

Sticking your face in the mud might sound like terrible health advice, but mud has been used for beauty and healing purposes for thousands of years! Today, some people even travel to fancy spas for mud facials or mud baths to soak up minerals that are supposedly good for your skin. But are they? Short answer: Yes, some are. Mud, especially mud from certain places like the Dead Sea, a saltwater lake in Asia, is jam-packed with minerals like salt and magnesium which can help keep your skin in tip-top shape.

Are ice baths dangerous?

What used to be mostly something just professional athletes did is now becoming more common: taking a dip in a nice icy bath to give your body a boost. But is swimming with the cubes really good for you? Or is it dangerous? Yes, and well, it can be. Athelete's use ice baths for good reason: They reduce inflammation in sore muscles. That's because when you take an icy plunge, your blood vessels constrict (get smaller) as your blood moves to the center of your body to try to keep your organs warm. When you exit the water and your temperature rises, your blood rushes back to the parts of your body in need of attention, taking nutrients and oxygen with it. But super cold temperatures can be risky. You can get burns from the ice; your body can go into shock; or you can get hypothermia, where your body temperature drops too low and puts your organs in danger. Ice baths are not always recommended for kids. If you're thinking about taking the plunge, do so under the guidance of a medical professional!

WILD WEATHER 53

Can bad weather make my grades better?

What do pop quizzes and thunderstorms have in common? They can both appear unexpectedly to ruin a perfectly nice day. But it's also possible one could give your brain a much-needed boost to help you with the other. According to some studies, bad weather may make you a better student! The reason? Gray days can suppress the happy hormones in your brain. That might sound like a bad thing, but this clears your mind of distraction, allowing you to think a little more deeply and remember things better. Also, when it's sunny and the feel-good hormones are pumping, your brain tends to think that everything is fine and go on autopilot. Your thoughts wander to other things, like what you'd prefer to be doing rather than being stuck inside studying! You heard it here, folks, bad weather = good grades!

What's so great about windmills?

When looking for clean sources of energy, experts turned to some pretty ancient technology. Windmills have been around since the eighth or ninth century! But did you know these massive fans can do much more than just harness the wind? They can actually help you breathe better by offering an alternative to fossil fuels. When humans burn coal and oil as their main source of energy, it releases pollutants like carbon and sulfur dioxide into the air. These pollutants can make it pretty hard to breathe. More and more people are turning to the sun and the wind as natural ways to power up their homes. Windmills are especially handy in places like Antarctica, which experiences months with no sunlight, which means no solar power. Wind, on the other hand, is always in season!

ASK SCARLETT

Is being outside ever bad for you?

As great as the great outdoors can be, there's a time and place for everything. And sometimes, that place might be on a cozy couch right in your own home—*especially* if there's an air quality alert. The Air Quality Index (AQI) measures the amount of pollutants in the air.

Of the five types of pollutants measured, one you might hear more and more about is called particle pollution: teeny-tiny, little specks of chemicals, mold spores, metals, and more floating through the air, ready to invade a nose near you. In fact, they're so small, your body's natural filters such as your skin and the mucus inside your nose are pretty useless against them. Don't worry, there are ways to mostly avoid them. Stay indoors on bad air quality days, and if you have to go out, try to wear a face mask! But why is particle pollution becoming such a familiar foe? It's the main ingredient in smoke from wildfires, which are on the rise all around the world.

WHY ARE MORE WILDFIRES HAPPENING?

In the past 20 years, wildfires around the globe have doubled, and experts say they will become even more frequent. Why? Blame climate change. Since Earth is becoming warmer and weather patterns have shifted, higher temperatures and periods with no rain are becoming more common. Without enough water to feed the plants and trees, they become dry and brittle; one little spark and a whole landscape might go up in flames. What to do about it? Well, for starters, even though these fires are wild, most are started by humans. Learning about fire safety and prevention is one of the best things you can do! But also, experts are figuring out how to fight fire with fire—literally. They burn up dead trees and plants in a controlled fire, so when a wild one breaks out, there will be nothing to fuel it—stopping the spread before it starts!

WILD WEATHER

What do I do when I feel bad about climate change?

It's hard to go anywhere these days without hearing about climate change and its effects: rising sea levels, wildfires, drought, and rising temperatures. And for the most part, that's a *good thing*—talking leads to action! But what happens to your brain when you want to save the planet, but you're starting to feel like you're carrying the weight of the world on your shoulders? Is climate change taking a toll on your mental health?

First, let's talk about what it is: **Climate change** means shifts in Earth's temperature and weather patterns. It's happened before (during the last Ice Age 2.6 million to 11,000 years ago), and it's happening now. The difference is that this time humans are the ones causing it.

ASK SCARLETT

For the past 200 years, people have used oil and coal to power machinery such as engines and factories. The burning of those fossil fuels releases gases into the atmosphere, which act like a warm blanket to heat the Earth. The increase is only about 1.9 degrees F, but it's enough to make the weather go wonky.

Eco-anxiety describes the hopeless feeling that some people have about solving the climate problem. For many, it feels like too big of an of an issue to tackle, and like one individual person could never make a difference.

If you've ever felt this way, there *are* things you can do!

➤ Look for news about the positive changes people are making, like a local beach cleanup near you, new technology that's cleaning oceans, or new sources of green energy.

➤ It's always easier with a team, and talking about your concerns with like-minded people can help. And maybe even find out what changes you can start making.

➤ Lean into all the ways nature can help your mental health. Go for a nature walk, meditate, listen to the sound of waves—whatever floats your boat! It will help you feel grounded and resilient and ready to fight for the planet!

WILD WEATHER

Why do I feel better in the summer?

Ah, summer. There's nothing I like better than stretching out in a nice shady patch of grass on a hot July day and taking a little snooze. That is, of course, unless that day turns into a real scorcher! But how high do those temps have to rise to stop being healthy and start giving you the summertime blues?

The summer is your brain's time to shine. Soaking in all that vitamin D from the sun, your brain is active, healthy, and getting extra doses of feel-good hormones. And outdoor time usually means playtime, especially if you're on a break from school. When you're moving your body, you are breathing more deeply, and your brain produces happy chemicals that make you feel like a million bucks. To top it all off, sweat can help fight bacteria, expel tiny amounts of toxins, make your skin glow, and prevent you from getting sick. What more could you want?

Don't say more heat! Extreme heat—the kind where temperatures soar above 90 degrees F—can be a problem. On a super-hot day, it's more difficult to manage normal body functions like **blood pressure** and even kidney and lung activity. When you sweat too much, your body gets dehydrated, and many people don't rehydrate well enough. More people go to the hospital with illnesses caused by heat than by any other weather-related event!

Kids' bodies are much better at handling the heat than grown-ups', but that doesn't mean you don't have to be careful. If you're out in hot temps, don't forget: wear sunscreen, try to seek out shade, and drink plenty of water.

Why does winter make me sleepy?

If the thought of a wintry day makes you want to curl up with some cocoa and a book by the fire, you're not alone. There's something about winter that sends your body into a sort of hibernation mode. Really! According to one survey, 58% of people said they were less active in the winter months. And that might be where the healing comes in.

When there's less to do, people tend to sleep more. Also, it doesn't hurt that when the temperature is cooler, it's easier to fall asleep more quickly. Researchers report that people get an average of 30 minutes more deep, sleep in the winter time because they snooze longer. Deep sleep is also called rapid eye movement sleep, or **REM** sleep, and is the phase of sleep in which your brain is active, you dream, your memories from the day are stored away, and your brain processes information. Without this phase of sleep, your brain doesn't get the rest it deserves. Go ahead, hit the snooze button! Your brain just may need it.

HEALTH HACK
Need an extra dose of confidence? Check the weather forecast!

Not only does the sun make you happy, it also might make you take more risks! The thinking behind this is simple: When you're in a better mood, you are more optimistic. You might take a chance on something unknown, because you believe the outcome will be positive. Researchers took a look at adult behaviors like buying lottery tickets, investing in the stock market, or shopping for cars. People do all three more when the weather is sunny (especially if it's unexpectedly sunny in an otherwise dreary month!). So the next time you make a bold move, check the weather—did the sun help you out?

WILD WEATHER

Does the full moon make people act weird?

You have probably heard stories about strange events occurring under the glow of a full moon: more babies are born, people act silly, some people transform into werewolves. Rest assured: none of these—especially not the last one—are true! It's a fact that the moon has a huge effect on planet Earth. It controls the ocean tides, influences animal migration patterns, and of course brightens up our night sky. But it has no real effect on human behavior that science can prove. It's possible there are some ways it can influence the human body, including blood pressure and sleep, but so far, after a lot of research, the science shows that people act the same whether the moon is a crescent, or full. *Phew!* I was always a little worried about that werewolves thing...

Is it weird to love winter?

Step aside summer! We've talked a lot about how warm weather chases the blues away, but what about people who like to chill out in the chill months? Whether you love winter, summer, fall, or spring has a lot to do with where and how you were raised. If you're from Colorado and love to hit the slopes, the winter months are probably your jam. If you're from Michigan, where winters can be bitterly cold but you spend summer on the beautiful lakes, you might be a summer kid. If you're from the East Coast of the United States, where summers are hot and humid and winters are cold and dreary, spring and fall might be your favorite times. Heading into your least favorite months with a positive mindset can make all the difference, according to research. If we believe something negative, we are more likely to feel negatively. But if we believe something positive, we are more likely to feel positively. So instead of focusing on how freezing or meltingly hot it's going to be, get excited for cozy hot cocoa or a fun pool day!

ASK SCARLETT

Weather-Wary

Do you ever hear a big clap of thunder and go running to the safety and security of your nearest loved one? It's hard not to—weather can be scary. Although meteorologists try their best to **forecast**, or predict, weather patterns and events, it's not easy to determine what the weather is going to actually do. And it's human nature to fear the unknown. Here are some common weather-related phobias and what they mean:

➤ **Astraphobia:** Fear of thunderstorms. This super-common problem affects humans and your furry friends!

➤ **Chionophobia:** Fear of snow. This fear centers around the dangerous conditions caused by snow, like falling on slippery sidewalks or bad driving conditions.

➤ **Ancraophobia:** Fear of wind. This fear might affect people who are reminded of destructive wind events in their lives.

➤ **Lilapsophobia:** Fear of extreme weather. This fear is usually about hurricanes and tornados, but it can also apply to violent thunderstorms.

➤ **Thermophobia:** Fear of heat. This fear is not only about hot weather but also hot things like a pan on a stove.

WILD WEATHER

Make a Rainstick!

In desperate need of some calm study time? Sounds like you could use a nice, dark, cloudy, rainy day! Too bad the forecast looks bright and sunny. Don't worry—Scarlett to the rescue! We can bring the rain to you—er—the sound of it, at least. Here's how you can make a simple rainstick at home:

Materials Needed:

- Paper towel roll
- Aluminum foil
- Uncooked rice
- Clear tape
- Paper
- Broom
- Large kitchen spoon

Step 1: Tear a foil sheet about 12 inches long. Twist it into a worm-like shape. Wrap it around the handle of a broom to form a spiral.

Step 2: Tear a second foil sheet about 8 inches long. Twist it into a worm-like shape. Wrap it around the handle of a large kitchen spoon to form a tighter spiral than the first. Insert the small spiral inside of the big spiral.

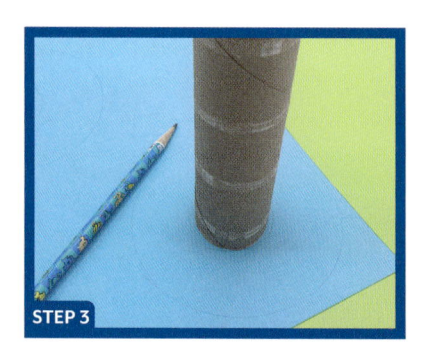

Step 3: Place the paper towel roll on the paper and trace the circle around the end (do this twice, one for each end). Now draw circles around your first circles, about two inches larger.

Step 4: Using the outermost lines as a guide, cut out your circles. Then, make about 12 cuts on each circle from the outer to the inner lines, forming "petals."

Step 5: Cover one end of the paper towel roll with a paper circle. Fold the petals around the sides of the tube, and tape to secure.

Step 6: Insert your foil spirals inside the tube.

Step 7: Carefully pour ¼ cup of uncooked rice into the tube.

Step 8: Cover the other end of the paper towel roll with your other paper circle. Fold the petals around the sides of the tube, and tape to secure.

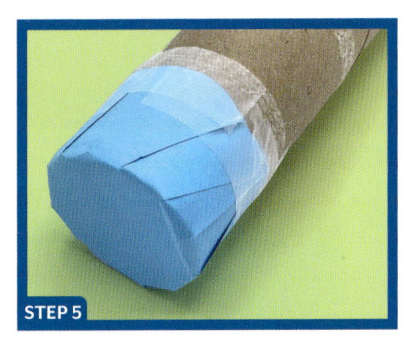

STEP 5

STEP 6

STEP 7

STEP 8

Step 9: Use colored pencils and paint to decorate your rainstick!

Now tip it upside down, and be prepared to relax to the sound of a "rainstorm."

WILD WEATHER   63

CHAPTER 5

Worldwide Wonders

Do certain places have special powers?

If you're like me, there's nothing you love more than a trip to a new place. And there's no doubt a quick getaway can help a tired brain get some much-needed rest. But when you're planning your next vacation, is it possible to pick a place that heals your mind and your body?

64   ASK SCARLETT

Wellness travel is a big deal—and I'm not just talking spas and resorts (though I enjoy a nice *paw*dicure as much as the next fox). I mean healing holes, wellness springs, volcanic facials—Earth's natural health spas. Do they really work?

It depends. Many of these hot spots make claims about healing powers that seem too good to be true, because, well, they are. If you want to attract tourists, you have to make it sound good, right? But in other spots, scientists believe there are real reasons people may pick up some good vibrations. Either way, getting out in nature is good for the mind and body, whether the "claim to fame" is true or not!

In this chapter, I'll whisk you around the world to sort the truth from the myths in search of the most epic vacation for your body and mind!

HEALTH HACK
Somewhere brand new—to you!

If you can't travel, have no fear! Even though it may not be the exotic destination of your dreams, your own backyard has plenty of exploring possibilities to offer. So before you beg your parents to take you halfway around the world in search of a "healing" forest, do some research and find an ecosystem you haven't explored yet closer to home. New to you might be just as good!

WORLDWIDE WONDERS 65

Energy Spots

Some people believe there are spots called **"energy vortices,"** where the Earth's energy swirls more powerfully than in other places. People have been seeking these spots for thousands of years as destination for healing, meditation, or spirituality. So are they real? Unfortunately, science says no. There's nothing special about these places that can be measured by science. But—they are often peaceful, quiet, and beautiful outdoor spaces. And by now we know how healing that can be, right?

The Healing Hole

In Bimini, the Bahamas there's a naturally fed freshwater pond in a saltwater mangrove forest— that's right, a pond in the middle of another body of water—that is famous for its "healing" powers. Its mineral-rich waters have been sought out by locals and tourists alike. But is there any truth to the claims? Looks like it! It turns out this mineral-rich hole is chock-full of lithium, sulfur, and magnesium. Lithium helps boost your happy hormones, magnesium helps make your muscles move and boosts your energy, and sulfur rebuilds your cells. You don't need to convince me, let's go!

Yakushima Island, Japan

Why head to Japan when you can natureb bathe pretty much anywhere? Because it's home to probably the most famous healing forest in the world. Over 20% of this island is covered in the greenest green space you'll ever see, with towering trees and moss-covered rocks, misty waterfalls, and glowing rivers. But that's not all that's special about Yakushima—it has sandy beaches, miles of rainforest, and 6,500-feet-tall mountain peaks! Because of this unique terrain, the biodiversity includes everything from monkeys to deer, crabs to cranes, sea turtles, bats, and more!

THE CAVE OF CRYSTALS

Although crystals may be not as helpful as we'd like here on Earth, is it possible they could help us discover something in a galaxy far, far away? For that answer we go to the Cave of Crystals in Mexico. The enormous cavern contains giant crystal beams measuring almost 40 feet tall—taller than most trees! But the hazardous cave conditions (it's about 136 degrees F and 90% humidity) make it tough to last even 10 minutes inside without special gear. This means anything living down there is an **extremophile**—an organism that can survive hostile conditions. Researchers have discovered dormant microbes, up to 50,000 years old, inside the crystals. And they were able to revive them!

Many scientists believe that when life on other planets is discovered, it will be adapted to living underground. Could unlocking the secrets of the crystal cave creatures help us befriend aliens?

WORLDWIDE WONDERS

The Blue Lagoon

Volcanoes have the power to heal—in a roundabout way. Just ask people who have visited the famous Blue Lagoon in Iceland. This manmade lagoon is located in a lava field with the closest active volcano less than two miles away! A **geothermal** powerplant harnesses this natural power to turn it into clean energy, and the Blue Lagoon is fed by the groundwater. The mineral-rich water, combined with a nice soothing temperature of about 100 degrees F, makes it the ultimate vacation for your skin! People go here to seek treatment for a number for skin disorders. There is even a line of Blue Lagoon beauty products!

The Grand Canyon

Have you ever been struck by the beauty of something so amazing, you feel it in your whole body? Well, apparently that feeling can help you live longer, according to some experts. Just looking out over an incredible sight like the Grand Canyon—a 277-mile-long, 18-mile-wide canyon that runs through the desert in Arizona—can signal your brain to release specific proteins in your body. These proteins tell your cells to amp up your immune system and blood cell production. That means, the more awe-inspiring the landscape, the healthier you'll be. Forget the vacation, just hand me a mirror!

The Dead Sea

With a name like that, you might think twice about visiting this healing hot spot—but don't let it fool you. First of all, the Dead Sea isn't a sea at all; it's a saltwater lake located in between Israel and Jordan. And travelers have been going there for centuries for very good reasons. It's one of the saltiest bodies of water on Earth—nine times saltier than the ocean! So you float because saltwater is denser than your body. Also because of the high salt content, it's hard for many creatures to survive, so you don't have to worry about deadly animals. Even the mud is healing: There is evidence that it has antibacterial properties, helping to treat acne and other skin ailments. The coolest thing though? Located 1,200 feet below sea level, the air is very hot and dry. As a result, the Dead Sea evaporates quickly! Because of this, there is something called an evaporation layer, a misty fog that hangs in the air, which filters out the sun's UV-A and UV-B rays. Swimmers can soak up vitamin D with less risk of burning.

SWIM AT YOUR OWN RISK!

Just because it's hard not to float in the Dead Sea doesn't mean you can't drown! In fact, it's one of the more dangerous bodies of water, because you *can't* sink! People claim the saltwater is so dense it's difficult to put your feet down and touch the bottom. Which is fine, as long as you're floating face up. If you accidentally get turned over, it's difficult to flip yourself back. That's why all of the hotels and spas located at the Dead Sea have plenty of lifeguards on duty at all times.

WORLDWIDE WONDERS

Is vacation good for you?

I don't know about you, but there's nothing I love more than a nice, long break from the daily grind. (Foraging for food can be exhausting!) And as you probably already know, it does your mind and body good to interrupt your regular routine every once in a while. Aside from the obvious benefits that come from a getaway to an exotic location—fun in the sun, activity, fresh air, or perhaps just catching up with grandma—there are a few unexpected reasons you could probably use some time off!

ASK SCARLETT

➤ **Reset that clock!** Did you know that your body keeps time? It's that circadian rhythm we talked about back in Chapter 1, and it's how your body keeps track of the 24 hours in a day: It tells you when to go to bed and when to wake up. Most people reset their natural circadian rhythms around their schedules, like by setting an alarm to get up and go to school. But, that reset means they often don't get the sleep they really need. At night, they do things like stare at screens, read, or do hobbies to catch up on relaxation time they feel like they missed during the day. Ignoring your circadian rhythm can make you feel sluggish, forgetful, and less happy. It might even keep you from healing as quickly from injury or illness. On vacation, you usually have a lot more free time. Sleep in! Ignore the clock and get back on your body's natural cycle.

➤ **Clear that clogged brain!** Stress at school and in everyday life can lead you to be tired, unable to focus, and unable to problem-solve. Going on vacation is like spring cleaning for your noggin and can actually make you a better student!

➤ **Be fit as a fiddle!** When your stress hormones go up, your body's natural disease shield goes down. That means the more frazzled you are, the likelier you are to get sick. Taking some time off not only heals your brain, it heals your body.

WORLDWIDE WONDERS

Does a staycation have the same benefits as a vacation?

Yes! You don't have to travel to relax. All of the reasons a vacation improves your health work for a staycation, too. The bottom line is that you need time off in order to keep your body and mind healthy and strong. No plane ticket? No problem! Create your dream getaway at home!

➤ **Clear your schedule:** Just because you're not traveling doesn't mean you can't enter total relaxation mode. Treat your staycation as if it were a trip and make sure everyone knows you are unavailable.

➤ **Make an itinerary:** Create a list of things you want to do and schedule them, just as you would on an actual trip. Is there a movie you want to see? Schedule it. A dessert you want to make? Put it on the list! The best way to get the most out of your staycation is to make it feel full of fun, relaxing experiences.

72 ASK SCARLETT

➤ **Set the mood:** Add some extra pillows and a comfy blanket to your bed. Hang some fairy lights for ambiance. Play some soothing music. Give yourself the five-star treatment.

➤ **Go sightseeing:** Face it, there's probably lots of cool stuff in your town you've probably never gotten around to doing—like bird-watching, meditating in a local park, or going on a picnic!. There's nothing better than discovering a gem in your own backyard.

➤ **Reconnect:** Catch up with family and friends. Go out to dinner with your family or cook an adventurous meal at home. Get ice cream with your pals. Sometimes we're all so busy with the hustle and bustle we forget to stop and appreciate the people around us.

➤ **Enjoy small moments:** Make a fancy smoothie, and relax in your backyard. Lay on a blanket and gaze at the stars. Grab some binoculars and check out the birds outside your window. Appreciate the little things. It makes the big things seem more manageable.

WORLDWIDE WONDERS

Glossary

Amygdala: the part of your brain that processes emotions

Anxiety: a feeling of unease, worry, or fear

Aromatherapy: the use of fragrant essential oils that some people believe heals the body

Bacteria: single-celled living organism; can cause sickness, but many are beneficial to your body

Barometric pressure: the amount of pressure in the atmosphere

Biomimicry: the design of materials or structures that are modeled after the natural world

Blood pressure: the amount of force that pushes blood through your heart

Blue space: a natural or manmade environment featuring water

Central nervous system: the brain, spinal cord, and nerve tissues that work together to make your body move

Chemosignaling: chemical signals given off by your body

Circadian rhythm: the 24-hour cycle that makes up your body's internal clock and tells you when to be asleep and when to be awake

Eco-anxiety: a feeling of helplessness and worry about climate change

Endorphins: a group of chemicals released from the brain that block pain and increase feelings of happiness

Energy vortices: places where energy is entering or exiting planet Earth

Empathy: care and concern for the well-being of others, including animals and the planet.

Extremophile: an organism that lives in extreme conditions

Geothermal: describing energy produced by the internal heat of Earth that can be harnessed as a renewable power source

Green space: a natural or manmade environment featuring plant life

Haptic memory: sensory memory related to touch

Hippocampus: the part of the brain associated with memory

Hormones: chemical substances that act like messengers in your body to help control how your cells and organs do their work

Immune system: the network of organs, blood cells, and tissues in your body that help fight infection and disease

Ions: a molecule with a positive or negative electrical charge

Magnetotactic bacteria: bacteria that reacts to Earth's magnetic field

Microbes: a tiny organism that can only be seen with a microscope

Nature bathing: intentional and extended sensory engagement with nature

Neurons: a type of cell that sends and receives messages between the body and brain

Olfactory bulb: the part of the brain that interprets smell

Papillae: when referring to the tongue, the little bumps that help grip food and contain tastebuds

Particle pollution: a mixture of solid and liquid droplets in the air

Petrichor: the smell of the earth after it rains

Pollinator: an insect or animal that carries pollen between two parts of the flower or between multiple plants to help the plant reproduce

Prosthetics: an artificial body part

Seasonal Affective Disorder (SAD): a mood disorder associated with the seasons that causes depression

UV-A rays and UV-B rays: ultraviolet rays from the sun that are necessary for vitamin D production and plant growth but can also be damaging to the skin

Virus: an infectious microbe that attaches itself to a living cell and replicates inside a body to cause illness

Resources

Websites

National Geographic Kids: kids.nationalgeographic.com
Ranger Rick: rangerrick.org

Books

All the Feelings Under the Sun by Leslie Davenport (2021)
Big Brain Book by Leanne Boucher Gill (2021)
Get Outside Guide by Nancy Honovich (2014)
Sensational Animal Senses by Leanne Boucher Gill (2024)
What to Do When Climate Change Scares You by Leslie Davenport (2024)
Weird and Wonderful Nature by Ben Hoare (2023)

More Outdoor Resources

Children & Nature Network: childrenandnature.org
National Park Service: nps.gov
Sierra Club: sierraclub.org
US Forest Service: fs.usda.gov

Index

A

Aging, 28
Air
    and barometric pressure, 51
    cleaned by rain, 51
    cleaned by trees, 13, 16
    at higher elevations, 12
    indoor and outdoor, 10, 20
Air pollution, 54, 55
Air Quality Index (AQI), 55
Alligators, 28–29
Amygdala, 43, 74
Ancraophobia, 61
Animals, 22–35. *See also individual animals*
    baby animal photos, 27
    and biomimicry, 31
    language in, 32–33
    learning from, 28–31
    pets, 23. *See also* Pets
    petting, 23, 35
    stuffed, 41
    therapy and emotional support, 34–35
Animal therapy, 23
Anxiety, 74
    eco-anxiety, 57, 74
    and weighted blankets, 40
AQI (Air Quality Index), 55
Arctic ground squirrel, 29
Aromatherapy, 36–37, 74
Astraphobia, 61

B

Bacteria, 74
    magnetotactic, 30
    microbes, 25
    petrichor caused by, 39
Barometric pressure, 51, 52, 74
Beach, relaxing effect of, 12
Bees, 24
Biomimicry, 31, 74
Bird-watching, 26
Blankets, weighted, 40
Blood pressure, 58, 74
Blood sugar, 46

Blue Lagoon, 68
Blue space(s), 17, 74
    and dolphin therapy, 27
    indoors, 21
    for pet fish, 26
Boundaries, 40
Brain-controlled prosthetics, 30
Brains
    insect, 25
    octopus, 30
Breathing, 10, 12

C

Calming effects of nature, 13
Cats, 22, 39
Cave of Crystals, 66
Central nervous system, 37, 74
CETI project (Cetacean Translation Initiative), 33
Chemosignaling, 39, 74
Chionophobia, 61
Circadian rhythm, 9, 71, 74
Cities, green spaces in, 16
Climate change, 55–57
Clothing, weighted, 40
Colds, 10, 38
Cold temperature, moods associated with, 19
Color theory, 44
Communication
    among trees, 13
    by dogs, 32
    languages, 32–33
Companion pets, intelligence of, 32
Crystal healing, 11

D

Dead Sea, 69
Diabetes, 26
Diaphragm, 10
Diet, balanced, 46
Dogs, 22, 23, 32, 39
Dolphins, 27
Dolphin therapy, 27
Drought, 13

E

Earth
    moon's effect on, 60
    smell of, 39, 51
Earthworms, 24
Eastgate Centre, 31
Eco-anxiety, 57, 74
Emotional support animals, 34–35
Emotions. *See also specific emotions*
    assigned to textures, 45
    and colors, 44
    and hunger, 46
    in insects, 25
    smell of, 39
    and smells, 37, 38
    sounds' effects on, 43
Empathy, 13
Endorphins, 13, 74
Energy
    from blood sugar, 46
    in crystals, 11
    from fossil fuels, 54, 57
    geothermal, 68, 74
    and mood, 19
    from windmills, 54
Energy vortices, 66–69
Erosion, 13
Essential oils, 37
Extremophile, 67, 74

F

Fear, smell of, 39
Fight-or-flight mode, 43
Fish, pet, 26
Food
    mood affected by, 46, 47
    pollination of, 24
    taste of, when sick, 38
Forest bathing, 48
Fossil fuels, 54, 57
Fresh air, 10, 20
Full moons, 60

INDEX

G

Geothermal energy, 68, 74
Germs, in indoor air, 10
Gorillas, 33
Grades, weather and, 54
Grand Canyon, 68
Grass, walking barefoot on, 11
Green spaces, 16, 20, 74
Grounding, 11

H

Happiness, 38, 39, 44
Haptic memory, 45, 74
Headaches, weather-related, 51
Healing
    rocks and crystals for, 11
    sleep for, 59
    travel locations for, 66–69
    wellness travel for, 65
Hearing, 42–43, 49
Heat
    deflected by plants, 16
    fear of, 61
    moods associated with, 19
    in summer, 58
    when you have a cold, 10
Hippocampus, 42, 75
Hippopotamuses, 31
Hormones, 75
    and bird-watching, 26
    on gray vs. on sunny days, 54
    at healing holes, 66
    from hugs, 40
    and immunity, 71
    and nature sounds, 43
    stress, 9, 23, 26, 43, 71
    and textures, 45
    when outside, 9
    when petting animals, 23, 35
    when stargazing, 18
Horses, miniature, 34
Hugs, 40
Humidity, 52
Hunger, 46
Hyaluronic acid, 28
Hypothermia, 53

I

Ice baths, 53
Immune system, 10, 68, 71, 75
Infection, 18, 29, 37
Insects, 24, 25
Intelligence
    of animals, 32–33
    of companion pets, 32
    of insects, 25
    of octopuses, 30
Ions, 75
    negative, 50
    positive, 18

K

Kangaroos, 29
Koko, 33

L

Languages, 32–33
Light
    from the sun, 21
    ultraviolet, 15, 69, 75
Lilapsophobia, 61
Lithium, 66
Llamas, 35
Longevity, 28

M

Magnesium, 53, 66
Magnetotactic bacteria, 30, 75
Marsupials, 29
Meditative state, 12, 51
Memory
    haptic, 45, 74
    and smells, 38
    textures triggering, 45
Mental health. *See also* Mood
    and bird's chirping, 26
    nature and, 57
    and negative ions, 50
    and scent memories, 38
Mice, 28
Microbes, 75
    in crystal caves, 67
    in your body, 25
Migration, by sea turtles, 30
Mind, clear, 12
Mindset, 60
Mineral water, 66, 68, 75
Miniature horses, 34
Miniature pigs, 35

Mood
    and being with animals, 22
    and blood sugar, 46
    foods' effects on, 46, 47
    and smells, 36, 37
    on staycations, 73
    in summer, 58
    and talking to pets, 33
    temperatures outside associated with, 19
    and weather forecast, 59
Moon, effect of, 60
Mountain climbing, 12
Mud, 53, 69

N

Naked mole rats, 28
Natural light, 21
Nature, 8–21. *See also specific elements of nature*
    at the beach, 12
    blue spaces, 17
    feeling better when in, 8–9
    green spaces, 16
    and health, 10–11
    to make you a better person, 13
    and mental health, 18, 57
    mountain climbing, 12
    sounds of, 42–43
    trees in, 13
    vitamin D from the sun, 14–15
    when indoors, 20–21
Nature bathing, 48, 67, 75
Neurons, 30, 75
Noise pollution, 16

O

Octopuses, 30
Olfactory bulb, 38, 75
Outside time. *See also* Nature
    during air quality alerts, 55
    to de-stress, 8–9
    endorphins released by, 13
    to help prevent colds, 10
    relaxation during, 47
    in summer, 58
Oxygen, 12, 13

P

Papillae, 47, 75
Parrots, 32, 33
Particle pollution, 51, 55, 75
Petrichor, 39, 51, 75

Pets
    companion, 32
    fish, 26
    responsibilities of owning, 35
    sleeping with, 23
    talking to, 33
Photosynthesis, 13
Pigs, miniature, 35
Plants
    green spaces, 16, 20, 74
    indoors, 20
    as living organisms, 13
    noise pollution reduced by, 16
    trees, 13, 16
Pollinators, 24, 75
Prosthetics, brain-controlled, 30

R

Rain, 50–51
Rainstick, making a, 62–63
Rats, 28, 35
Red blood cells, 12
Relaxation
    at the beach, 12
    from indoor natural elements, 21
    outdoors, 47
    on staycations, 72–73
    on vacations, 71
Repetitive sounds/touch, 51
Rest-and-digest mode, 47
Rocks, health benefits of, 11

S

SAD (Seasonal Affective Disorder), 19, 75
Saltwater, 69
Screens
    images of nature on, 21
    time spent on, 9
Seasonal Affective Disorder (SAD), 19, 75
Sea turtles, 30
Senses, 36–49
    hearing, 42–43, 49
    hunger, 46
    sight, 44, 48
    smell, 36–39, 49
    taking in the environment through, 48–49
    taste, 38, 46–47, 49
    touch, 40–41, 45, 49
    when you are relaxed, 47
Service animals, 34
Sight, 44, 48
Skin, 53, 68

Sleep
    after spending time outdoors, 9
    and bird-watching, 26
    importance of, 9
    with pets, 23
    REM, 59
    soothings sounds for, 42–43
    with stuffed animals, 41
    in winter, 59
Smell, 36–39, 49
Snakes, 34
Snow, 52, 61
Sounds of nature, 42–43
Sperm whales, 33
Squirrels, 29
Stargazing, 18
Staycations, 72–73
Storms, 51, 52, 61
Stress
    effect of nature on, 8–9
    fight-or-flight mode with, 43
    and scent memories, 38
    and screentime, 9
    and vacations, 71
Stuffed animals, 41
Summer, 58
Sun
    circadian rhythm supported by, 9
    hippos' protection from, 31
    immune system boosted by, 10
    light from the, 21
    and mood, 19, 59
    ultraviolet radiation from, 15
    vitamin D from, 10, 14–15
Sunscreen, 14, 15, 31
Supertasters, 47
Sweat, 31, 39, 58

T

Taste, 38, 46–47, 49
Tastebuds, 38, 47
Temperature, body, 29, 53
Temperature, outdoor
    and ability to sleep, 59
    and climate change, 57
    moods associated with, 19
    and termite homes, 31
Termites, 31
Textures, 45
Therapy animals, 34–35
Thermophobia, 61
Thinking
    on gray vs. on sunny days, 54
    by octopuses, 30
    positive and negative mindsets, 60

Tickling, 41
Touch, 40–41, 45, 49
Travel
    vacations, 70–71
    for wellness, 65–69
Trees, 13, 16

U

UV-A rays, 15, 69, 75
UV-B rays, 15, 69, 75

V

Vacations, 70–71
Viruses, 10, 75
Vitamin D, 10, 14–15
Volcanoes, 68

W

Walking barefoot outside, 11
Water. *See also* Blue space(s)
    blue spaces, 17, 21
    health benefits of, 17
    ice baths, 53
    mineral-rich, 66, 68
Weather, 50–61
    and climate change, 55–57
    and grades, 54
    phobias about, 61
    rain, 50–51
    scary, 61
    storms, 51, 52, 61
    in summer, 58
    in winter, 59
Weather forecasts, 59, 61
Weighted blankets/clothing, 40
Wellness travel, 65
White blood cells, 11
Wildfires, 55
Windmills, 54
Winds, 18, 50, 61
Winter, 59, 60
Wolves, 46

Y

Yakushima Island, Japan, 67

Photo Credits

Cover
(u), dugdax/Shutterstock
(cl), andreswd/iStock
(bl), Sally Cullen, National Wildlife Federation (2016)
(r), Max Topchii/Shutterstock

Front Matter
4, Marya Mchaffie, National Wildlife Federation (2008)
6, Sam Parks, National Wildlife Federation (2016)

Chapter 1
8 (u), takayuki/Shutterstock
9, (u), Anchiy/iStock
9, (b), Fertnig/iStock
10 (u), courtneyk/iStock
10 (b), Elizabeth Eldridge, National Wildlife Federation (2016)
11 (u), Sebastian Janicki/Shutterstock
11 (b), New Africa/Shutterstock
12 (u), Iakov Kalinin/Shutterstock
12 (b), Pollyana Ventura/iStock
13 (u), Rick Kramer, National Wildlife Federation (2014)
13 (b), IM_photo/Shutterstock
14 (ul), Yuri A/Shutterstock
14 (ur), Prokrida/Shutterstock
14 (b), Photoongraphy/Shutterstock
15 (u), MaeManee/Shutterstock
16, Nicholas J Klein/Shutterstock
17, Marc Dufresne/iStock
18 (u), S Curtis/Shutterstock
18 (b), Andrey Prokhorov/Shutterstock
19, BlueSkyImage/Shutterstock
20, Gita Kulinitch Studio/Shutterstock
21 (u), xxmmxx/iStock
21 (u, screen inset), Joe Schmitt, National Wildlife Federation (2015)
21 (b), sophiecat/Shutterstock

Chapter 2
22 (cl), Nynke van Holten/Shutterstock
22 (cr), fizkes/Shutterstock
23 (u), vitapix/iStock
23 (l), Dmitry Kalinovsky/Shutterstock
24 (u), Mark Brinegar, National Wildlife Federation (2015)
24 (b), Nick N A/Shutterstock
25 (u), Elif Bayraktar/Shutterstock
25 (b), Deborah Roy, National Wildlife Federation (2021)
26 (u), mauriziobiso/iStock
26 (b), Randy Streufert, National Wildlife Federation (2016)
27 (u), Sokolov Alexey/Shutterstock
27 (b), Volodymyr Burdiak/Shutterstock
28, Eric Isselee/Shutterstock
29 (u), Mark_Kostich/Shutterstock
29 (c), Dawn Wilson Photo/Shutterstock
29 (b), Anan Kaewkhammul/Shutterstock
30 (u), BirdImages/iStock
30 (b), Abbypphotos/Shutterstock
31 (u), Henk Bogaard/Shutterstock
31 (cl), Piotr Gatlik/Shutterstock
31 (bl), Carlos Takudzwa Kankhungwa/iStock
32, GlobalP/iStock
33 (u), Grafissimo/iStock
33 (b), Valerie Laney, National Wildlife Federation (2017)
34 (u), Alexia Khruscheva/Shutterstock
34 (b), GlobalP/iStock
35 (u), jensenwy/iStock
35 (b), Luvtinytoes/Shutterstock

Chapter 3
36, Denis Kuvaev/Shutterstock
37 (u), Cincinart/Shutterstock
37 (c), Avocado_studio/Shutterstock
37 (cru), inacio pires/Shutterstock
37 (crb), jaojormami/Shutterstock
37 (bl), Vera Larina/Shutterstock
37 (br), Armas Vladimir/Shutterstock
38 (u), Annavish/Shutterstock
38 (b), Naaz Stock/Shutterstock
39 (u), Kichigin/Shutterstock
39 (b), Ground Picture/Shutterstock
40 (u), fizkes/Shutterstock
40 (b), Trong Nguyen/Shutterstock
41 (u), Ralers/iStock
41 (b), StockPlanets/iStock
42 (u), Lisa-S/Shutterstock
42 (b), PANDECH/Shutterstock
43 (u), Karel Zahradka/Shutterstock
43 (c), manve/iStock
43 (b), Minerva Studio/Shutterstock
45 (u), beton studio/Shutterstock
45 (b), jarabee123/Shutterstock
46 (u), Spirit9/Shutterstock
46 (b), Tatevosian Yana/Shutterstock
47 (u), Monkey Business Images/Shutterstock
47 (c), OllyDark/Shutterstock
47 (b), Viktorya Telminova/Shutterstock
48, sun ok/Shutterstock
49, William H. Wiley, National Wildlife Federation (2007)

Chapter 4
50 (u), TORWAISTUDIO/Shutterstock
50 (b), Vita Olivko/Shutterstock
51 (u), muratart/Shutterstock
51 (b), phive/Shutterstock
52 (u), Andrey Skutin/Shutterstock
52 (b), VAWiley/iStock
53 (u), Studio Romantic/Shutterstock
53 (b), evaurban/Shutterstock
54 (u), Torychemistry/Shutterstock
54 (b), hrui/Shutterstock
55 (u), Mikhail Gnatkovskiy/Shutterstock
55 (b), Alaskagirl8821/Shutterstock
56, Triff/Shutterstock
57 (u), TR STOK/Shutterstock
57 (c), VH-studio/Shutterstock
57 (b), jacoblund/iStock
58, Lauren Ames, National Wildlife Federation (2021)
59 (u), Michael Burrell/iStock
59 (b), Brocreative/Shutterstock
60 (u), Klagyivik Viktor/Shutterstock
60 (b), Olya Humeniuk/Shutterstock
61 (u), Steve Allen/Shutterstock
61 (c), djgis/Shutterstock
61 (b), Jonah Lange/Shutterstock
62-63, Chris Gaugler

Chapter 5
64, Panos Laskarakis, National Wildlife Federation (2013)
65 (u), Steve Perry, National Wildlife Federation (2015)
65 (b), Here Now/Shutterstock
66, LittleWindowsOfTheWorld/Shutterstock
67 (u), Nakasaku/Shutterstock
67 (b), Bambuh/Shutterstock
68 (u), Miroslav Denes/Shutterstock
68 (b), Amanda Mohler/Shutterstock
69, Joerg Steber/Shutterstock
70 (u), Jam Norasett/Shutterstock
70 (b), Reuben James/iStock
71 (u), Tom Merton/iStock
71 (b), Mumemories/iStock
72 (u), Edwin Tan/iStock
72 (b), kali9/iStock
73 (u), SolStock/iStock
73 (c), Yuri A/Shutterstock
73 (b), Lopolo/Shutterstock

Becky Baines is a children's book writer and editor and former editorial director at National Geographic Kids. She has written books for kids about topics from dogs to bones to eggs to spiders.

Books for Kids from APA
The American Psychological Association works to advance psychology as a science and profession, as a means to improve health and human welfare. APA publishes books for young readers under its imprint, Magination Press. It's the combined power of psychology and literature that helps kids navigate life's challenges a little easier. Visit maginationpress.org and @ Magination Press on Facebook, X, Instagram, and Pinterest.

The National Wildlife Federation, America's largest and most trusted conservation organization, works across the country to unite Americans from all walks of life in giving wildlife a voice. NWF has been on the front lines for wildlife since 1936, fighting for the conservation values that are woven into the fabric of our nation's collective heritage. NWF is also a publisher of magazines for children. For over 55 years, the *Ranger Rick* group of magazines has aimed to inspire in its readers a greater understanding of the natural world, a deep love of nature and wildlife, and a lasting commitment to conservation and environmental action.